WITHDRAWN

A Knight in a Fight

by Spencer Brinker

Consultant:
Beth Gambro
Reading Specialist
Yorkville, Illinois

Contents

BEARPORT
PUBLISHING

New York, New York

A Knight in a Fight

Freddy is a **knight** whose suit is too **tight**.

It doesn't fit **right** in the day or the **night**.

When a dragon is in **sight**, Freddy stands at full **height**.

He leans to
the **right**, and
waves his sword
with all his **might**.

"Go away, take **flight**! Or I will give you a **fright**!"

But there's never
a **fight**, just a
hot, fiery **light**.

It's hard to be a **knight** in a suit that's too **tight**!

Key Words in the -ight Family

fight

flight

height

knight

light

night

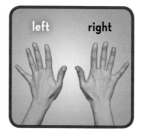
right

tight

Other **-ight** Words: **bight, delight, plight**

Index

About the Author

Spencer Brinker loves to tell "dad jokes"
and play word games with his twin girls.

Teaching Tips

Before Reading

✔ Introduce rhyming words and the **–ight** word family to readers.

✔ Guide readers on a "picture walk" through the text by asking them to name the things shown.

✔ Discuss book structure by showing children where text will appear consistently on pages. Highlight the supportive pattern of the book.

During Reading

✔ Encourage readers to "read with your finger" and point to each word as it is read. Stop periodically to ask children to point to a specific word in the text.

✔ Reading strategies: When encountering unknown words, prompt readers with encouraging cues such as:

- **Does that word look like a word you already know?**
- **Does it rhyme with another word you have already read?**

After Reading

✔ Write the key words on index cards.

- **Have readers match them to pictures in the book.**

✔ Ask readers to identify their favorite page in the book. Have them read that page aloud.

✔ Choose an **–ight** word. Ask children to pick a word that rhymes with it.

✔ Ask children to create their own rhymes using **–ight** words. Encourage them to use the same pattern found in the book.

Credits: Cover, © Rick Partington/Shutterstock and © Valentyna Chukhlyebova/Shutterstock; 2–3, © Iurii Stepanov/Shutterstock, © cigdem/Shutterstock, and © Kim Jones; 4, © Ralf Juergen Kraft/Shutterstock and © Kim Jones; 5, © GreenSprocket/Shutterstock, © Hurst Photo/Shutterstock, and © Kim Jones; 6–7, © Valentyna Chukhlyebova/Shutterstock and © Kim Jones; 8–9, © Valentyna Chukhlyebova/Shutterstock and © Kim Jones; 10–11, © Valentyna Chukhlyebova/Shutterstock and © Kim Jones; 12–13, © Iurii Stepanov/Shutterstock, © Iurii Stepanov/Shutterstock, and © Kim Jones; 14–15, © Valentyna Chukhlyebova/Shutterstock, © Iurii Stepanov/Shutterstock, and © Kim Jones; 16T (L to R), © Kim Jones, © Valentyna Chukhlyebova/Shutterstock, © 4zevar/Shutterstock, and © Kim Jones; 16B (L to R), © haveseen/Shutterstock, © GreenSprocket/Shutterstock, and © Iurii Stepanov/Shutterstock.

Publisher: Kenn Goin   **Senior Editor:** Joyce Tavolacci   **Creative Director:** Spencer Brinker

Library of Congress Cataloging-in-Publication Data: Names: Brinker, Spencer, author. | Gambro, Beth, consultant. Title: A knight in a fight / by Spencer Brinker; consultant: Beth Gambro, Reading Specialist. Description: New York, New York: Bearport Publishing, [2020] | Series: Read and rhyme: level 3 | Includes index. Identifiers: LCCN 2019007188 (print) | LCCN 2019010172 (ebook) | ISBN 9781642806120 (Ebook) | ISBN 9781642805581 (library) | ISBN 9781642807233 (pbk.) Subjects: LCSH: Readers (Primary) | Knights and knighthood—Juvenile fiction. Classification: LCC PE1119 (ebook) | LCC PE1119 .B75186 2020 (print) | DDC 428.6/2—dc23 LC record available at https://lccn.loc.gov/2019007188

10 9 8 7 6 5 4 3 2 1